instant gratification
candles

instant gratification
candles
FAST & FABULOUS PROJECTS

by Carol Endler Sterbenz & Genevieve A. Sterbenz | Photographs by Julie Toy

CHRONICLE BOOKS
SAN FRANCISCO

Copyright © 2001 Carol Endler Sterbenz and Genevieve A. Sterbenz.
Photographs copyright © 2001 Julie Toy.
Illustrations copyright © 2001 Nicole Kaufman.
All rights reserved. No part of this book may be reproduced in any form without written permission from the publisher.

Library of Congress Cataloging-in-Publication available.

ISBN: 0-8118-2853-0

Printed in Hong Kong

Candle Dust is a registered trademark of Glory Bee.
Candle Glass is a registered trademark of Pourette.
Rub 'n Buff is a registered trademark of Amaco.

The authors wish to thank Joe Dance at Crate & Barrel, Shannon Arch at Glory Bee Company,
and Ken Ptak at the Walnut Hill Company.
The photographer would like to thank Saadi Howell and Tracy Johnson.
Prop styling by Robbin Turk
Designed by Level, Calistoga, CA

Distributed in Canada by Raincoast Books
9050 Shaughnessy Street
Vancouver, British Columbia V6P 6E5

10 9 8 7 6 5 4 3 2 1

Chronicle Books LLC
85 Second Street
San Francisco, California 94105

www.chroniclebooks.com

This book is intended as a guide to the craft of candle-making. As with any craft project, it is important that all the instructions are followed carefully, as failure to do so could result in injury. Every effort has been made to present the information in this book in a clear, complete, and accurate manner, however not every situation can be anticipated and there can be no substitute for common sense. Check product labels, for example, to make sure that the materials you use are safe and nontoxic. Be careful when handling hot wax, as it can cause serious burns. And do not leave burning candles unattended. The authors and Chronicle Books disclaim any and all liability resulting from injuries or damage caused during the production or use of the craft candles discussed in this book.

table of

contents

introduction

There is little that rivals the atmosphere created by the glow of a lighted candle. The moment the wick of even the smallest taper candle flickers with a flame, the world changes from one of angles and edges to one of softness and calm. It is no wonder that in spite of the illumination that any electric light can supply, we are drawn to rooms lit with candlelight, rooms that become filled with the promise of romance, friendship, and celebration.

Instant Gratification: Candles is a sourcebook offering extraordinarily easy ways to decorate and make candles. The collection features more than 40 original ideas for transforming ordinary candles into exquisite design accents for every room of your home and for every occasion. Everything you need to know is included in the step-by-step instructions that accompany each exquisite design, pictured in a full-color, styled photograph.

In Chapters 1, 2, and 3, candle designs are based on decorating the exterior of already-made candles. Few approaches to candle making are more straightforward, and few methods are as easy to follow, even if you have no previous candle-making experience.

The candles featured in these chapters are meant to inspire you by introducing you to such decorative techniques as painting and glazing, as well as adding little accents that provide big impact. All the ideas are designed to be used on candles whose shapes you can easily find in stores—from big blocks and plump orbs to slender pillars and sculpted fruit-shaped candles.

For example, you can begin with a square pillar candle, adding decorative motifs by hand. Paint on foliage or flowers. Or, surround your candle with lanterns made of snowy parchment or wire mesh to create a lighting accent with a soft glow. Or, embellish your candles by applying found art. Consider a portrait candle where you glue on photocopied photographs of your family and friends. Or, instead, cut and glue colored paper squares in a mosaic pattern on your candle. Then, dip your decorated candles in a bath of melted wax. The glaze will preserve and protect the applied illustrations, while conferring a luminous quality to the chosen art.

In Chapters 4, 5, and 6, the candle designs are primarily those that require melted wax for their fabrication and their textural effects. While the shapes of some candles are created by using dipping and layering techniques, others are made by pouring and molding.

The most traditional of all techniques is dipping, where a taper-shaped candle is formed by repeatedly submerging a wick in melted wax until the desired thickness is reached. Perhaps the most popular and versatile way to make a candle is to use a mold. Molds are fun and easy to use because their three-dimensional shapes and character can be replicated perfectly in wax. You can find molds in your own home—consider an ordinary milk container. Pour melted wax into a recycled container, add several wicks, then let the wax harden. When you remove the candle, you will have a sophisticated multi-wick lighting accent.

Sometimes the beauty and charm of a finished candle comes from displaying the mold in which the candle is made. Imagine a candle housed in a delicately painted china cup, or one made in a hollowed-out lemon with a little ribbon handle. Peruse the candle designs that follow. You will find that making beautiful candles from scratch has never been so easy.

Instant Gratification: Candles will become a trusted companion and resident stylist. You will find that once you begin with any of the designs, you will look forward to using your imagination to make candles of your own design. A separate technical glossary is included to further help you along the way. You will be surprised and satisfied by the ease with which you can make these candles, which will accompany you during those moments in life when only candlelight will do.

- **Never leave a burning candle unattended.**

- **Keep open flames away from all flammable materials.**

- **Always place candles on a level, nonflammable surface.**

- **Keep children and pets away from lighted candles.**

- **Candles made in metal or glass containers can get hot. Use caution when handling them.**

- **Wear gloves and an apron, and use oven mitts, whenever handling hot wax.**

- **Always melt wax in the top half of a double boiler, never over an open flame. Never leave melting wax unattended.**

- **Monitor the temperature of wax very carefully. Do not allow the wax to reach temperatures above 215°F. It will smoke at approximately 250°F and ignite at 375°F.**

To put out a wax fire, turn off the heat source and smother the fire with a damp cloth, baking soda, or a metal pot lid. Treat it as you would cooking oil that ignites in a frying pan. **Do not put the fire out with water.**

Excess wax can be reused. Let it harden and reheat it at a later time for another project. Never pour hot wax down the drain.

To clean wax off utensils, chip off large pieces of wax. Run utensils or pots under hot water to soften wax and gently rub with steel wool to thoroughly remove any wax residue. Also, if a pot is filled with wax, try boiling water in it. Wax will melt and float to the top. Pour off wax/water.

The project you choose will determine the type and amount of wax as well as the thickness and length of the wick you will need to make a successful candle. These requirements will help ensure that candles will burn without smoking, dripping excessively, or self-extinguishing. Use the chart below to coordinate the elements so that you can design your own candles.

Paraffin Wax: For every $3\frac{1}{2}$ fluid ounces a mold holds, you need 3 ounces of cold wax. Melting point 129°F: Use for container-type candles and votives. Melting point 139°F: Use for overdipping. Melting point 140°F: Use for molds (metal, plastic, rubber, and free-form). Melting point 145°F: Use for tapers only.

Wicking: Square braid: Use for dipped and molded candles. Available in different widths for candles up to 2 inches in diameter, 2 to 4 inches in diameter, 4 to 6 inches in diameter, and 6 to 9 inches in diameter.

Flat braid wicking: Use for rolled candles. Available in different widths for candles up to 1 inch in diameter, 1 to 2 inches in diameter, and 2 to 4 inches in diameter.

Papercore wicking: Use for container-type candles or votives. Available in different widths for candles up to 2 inches in diameter, 2 to 4 inches in diameter, and 4 to 6 inches in diameter.

Stearin: One part stearin to ten parts wax (10 percent of wax mixture). Used to harden wax, curb dripping, and help release candles from molds.

Translucent Crystals (also known as Clear Sheen): $\frac{1}{4}$ teaspoon to 1 pound of wax. Used to harden wax and improve surface finish.

Color Chips: Number of chips determines how light or how dark the color of the wax is. Fewer chips produce a lighter color, more chips produce a darker color.

1

painted

Retro Daisies

Painting candles with floral motifs is one of the easiest ways to decorate them all over with a pretty pattern! For your next birthday party, you can create a sassy candle covered with daisies using simple brush strokes. All you do is brush on petals around a little center dot to make one bloom. Adding drops of liquid soap to the paint beforehand will help it adhere to the wax. If you prefer a more personalized candle, you can paint on the letters of someone's name, or the words of a sweet message that commemorates the special occasion in simple block letters.

YOU WILL NEED:

Aluminum pie tin

Acrylic paint in bright yellow
   and white

Liquid dishwashing soap

Paintbrush

5-inch-diameter round candle
   in light yellow

Cup of water

Paper towels

Candle Glass (optional)

1. In opposite corners of pie tin, pour a small pool of yellow and a small pool of white paint. Add one drop of soap to each pool of paint, and mix using paintbrush.

2. Dip paintbrush in yellow paint and make a small dot on the side of candle. Rinse brush in water and wipe brush clean on paper towel.

3. To make a petal, dip paintbrush in white paint. Press brush firmly against the surface and then lift it up gently as you complete the stroke; repeat action, painting remaining petals at even intervals in a radial pattern around yellow dot.

4. Repeat steps 2 and 3 to paint daisies in overall pattern, or as desired.

5. If desired, apply light coat of Candle Glass, following manufacturer's instructions.

Fortune Votives

Bring a little Asian flair into your home with these glowing votive accents. Each candle is decorated with a Chinese character and carries your heartfelt wishes of love, luck, and prosperity. The secret to forming each beautiful character is to use a paint pen designed specifically for wax. Next time you give a dinner party, place one decorated votive at each guest's place setting.

YOU WILL NEED:

4 round votive candles, each
   1 3/4 inches in diameter by 2 inches
   high, in gold or deep yellow
Pattern (page 107)
Pencil
Tracing paper
Scissors
Masking tape
Black paint marker for candles
1 1/4 inch–diameter round template,
   or lid from spice jar

1. To decorate candle side with one character, choose character from those shown on page 107; using pencil, trace character on paper. Using scissors, cut out traced character and center it on one side of candle. Secure with masking tape. Go over traced line of character using pencil, pressing in to dent wax slightly. Remove tracing paper and tape. Using paint marker, go over indented lines of character, thickening certain lines as indicated on pattern.

2. To finish, center circle template over painted character on candle, tracing around edge using paint pen.

3. Repeat steps 1 and 2 with remaining votive candles.

Bamboo Leaves

Sophisticated and beautiful, these leafy branches of bamboo suggest a foray into a tropical paradise. Decorated simply by wrapping a paper stencil around a candle and filling in the cutouts with green paint, this candle is perfect for exotic outdoor dinners.

YOU WILL NEED:

Pattern (page 107)

Self-healing mat

X-Acto knife

3-inch-square candle, 6 inches high,
  in white

Masking tape

Stencil paint in dark green

Disposable plastic lid

Liquid dishwashing soap

Stencil brush

Candle Glass (optional)

Note: You will need access to a black-and-white photocopy machine.

1. Photocopy pattern on page 107.

2. Lay pattern on self-healing mat. To create stencil, use X-Acto knife to cut along marked lines, removing cutouts.

3. Tightly wrap stencil around candle, aligning bottom edge of pattern with bottom of candle, and overlapping pattern at back. Secure with masking tape.

4. Pour small pool of paint onto plastic lid. Add one drop of soap to pool of paint and mix with stencil brush.

5. Dip brush in paint, then dab onto stencil, keeping paint within cutout shapes. Let paint dry.

6. Remove tape and stencil from candle.

7. If desired, apply light coat of Candle Glass, following manufacturer's instructions.

Constellation

Scatter sparkling stars across a silver background using ordinary stationery supplies and rub-on paint. All you need to do is press self-adhesive stars on the candle in a constellation of your own design. Then rub on silver paint and peel off the stickers. To add the texture and sparkle of new-fallen snow, sprinkle the candle with diamond dust. The particles will catch the light and make the entire candle shine.

YOU WILL NEED:

Self-adhesive stars, 1/2 inch wide

3-inch-diameter round candle,

   3 inches high, in white

1 tube Rub 'n Buff paint in silver

Cotton cloth

Straight pin

Kraft paper

Rubber gloves

Spray adhesive

4 tablespoons diamond dust

CAUTION: Handle diamond dust with care; it is made with tiny, sharp splinters of real glass.

1. Peel off stars from backing and adhere to candle in random overall pattern.

2. Squeeze dab of paint on finger and rub over surface of candle, adding more paint as necessary to completely cover surface of wax. Let paint dry.

3. To burnish paint on candle and remove excess paint, rub surface of candle with cloth.

4. To remove a star, carefully use pin to lift up one edge, then peel off entire star.

5. Repeat step 4 with remaining stars.

6. Place candle upside down on clean, flat work surface covered with Kraft paper.

7. While wearing rubber gloves, apply light, thin coat of spray adhesive to outside of candle. Wait 5 minutes or until glue is tacky.

8. Sprinkle diamond dust on outside of candle.

accented

2

Collage

The minimalist beauty of this candle decoration comes from the simple torn papers tied around the middle of a candle with a few strands of raffia. The two color-coordinated papers are each torn along their grain, leaving a naturally deckled edge. When the papers are layered together, staggered so one edge is slightly lower than the other, they create a visual echo that underscores the tranquility of the design.

2 pieces 11-inch-by-17-inch decorative

   paper in coordinating colors to

   match candle

Ruler

Pencil

4-inch square candle, 5 inches high,

   in color as desired

3 pieces of raffia, each 24 inches long

Scissors

1. Lay one piece of paper on top of the other on flat work surface and measure and mark out a 17-inch-by-1½-inch band from each of the papers. Lay ruler parallel to long side of marked band 2 inches below top edge of paper. Use one hand to press down ruler, and the other to pull up papers against edge of your ruler.

2. Lay one band of paper on top of the other, in a horizontal orientation, shifting top paper down so that it is ¼ inch lower than bottom paper. Hold bands together in this position and wrap them around "waist" of candle, overlapping ends at center of back side.

3. Secure bands by wrapping around with two or three strands of raffia, tying ends in double knot at front. Using scissors, trim ends of raffia.

Coordinating Cubes

It is so easy to coordinate a trio of store-bought candles by adding labels. Simply print narrow bands of paper with thoughtful messages or the monogram of the person for whom the candles are intended, and wrap them around three block-shaped candles. Place the trio together in a sleek gift box. You will be proud to present these candles to anyone on your gift list.

YOU WILL NEED:

Self-healing mat

Cardstock in white

Ruler

Pencil

X-Acto knife

**Rubber stamp with message
  or monogram**

Stamp pad in yellow

Embossing powder in clear

Scrap of paper

Heat gun

**3 square candles, each 3 inches wide
  by 3 inches high, in green**

High-tack white glue

1. On self-healing mat, measure, mark, and cut three 13-inch-by-$1\frac{1}{2}$-inch bands from cardstock, using ruler, pencil, and X-Acto knife. Set two bands aside.

2. For first band, press rubber stamp in pad and press stamp down on center of paper band. Sprinkle inked image with embossing powder, shaking off excess onto scrap of paper. Funnel extra powder back into container. Use heat gun to melt powder, waving heat gun over the image in an even sweeping motion.

3. Repeat step 2 with remaining two bands.

4. Center and wrap message band around "waist" of one candle, overlapping ends at center of back side. Use a dab of high-tack glue to secure overlap.

5. Repeat step 4 to affix bands to remaining candles.

Royal Seal

The aristocratic elegance of a wax seal is undeniable. Now you can decorate the front of any candle using a wax seal you have made yourself. All that is required is a "pencil" of sealing wax and a metal stamp of your choosing, available at most stationery stores. The process is super simple. It is done in two easy steps. Melt and drip a little pool of sealing wax on the front of your candle, then press in your design.

YOU WILL NEED:

3-inch square candle,
   3 inches high, in ivory

Pushpin

12 $\frac{1}{4}$-inch-long satin ribbon,
   $\frac{1}{4}$ inch wide

Pliers

2 straight pins, $\frac{1}{4}$ inch long

Taper candle

Candlestick

Matches

Sealing wax "pencil" in gold

Large stainless-steel spoon

Rubber gloves

Metal stamp with motif, as desired

1. On center of candle front, use pushpin to make set of crosshatches in a $\frac{1}{2}$-inch-square area. Wrap ribbon around candle, trimming ends so they meet at crosshatch. Use pliers to hold and push one straight pin into each end of ribbon. Set aside.

2. Set up taper candle in candlestick and light wick using match; lay square candle, with crosshatches facing up, on protected, flat work surface.

3. Crack off $\frac{1}{2}$-inch chunk of sealing wax from "pencil" and place in spoon.

4. Put on rubber gloves. Hold spoon over candle flame until wax melts.

5. Let wax cool slightly (about 12 to 15 seconds). While wax is still warm, position spoon with melted wax over ribbon ends and set of crosshatches on candle. Carefully tilt spoon to allow melted sealing wax to drip in contained 1-inch-diameter circle on ribbon candle. If wax slides out of shape, nudge with gloved finger to push it into a circle shape. Immediately press metal seal into center of wax circle, indenting wax with motif. Let wax cool.

Marbleized Paper Lantern

The beauty of this lantern made from marbleized vellum is accentuated when paired with a drinking glass that has an etched pattern. The juxtaposition of the vertical pleats of the lantern and the horizontal pattern on the glass is highlighted when the flickering tea light placed within the glass plays on the paper.

YOU WILL NEED:

Self-healing mat

2 sheets marbleized vellum,

   each 8 $^1/_2$ inches by 10 inches

Ruler

Pencil

X-Acto knife

High-tack white glue

Drinking glass, 3 $^1/_4$ inches in diameter,

   3 $^1/_4$ inches high with etched pattern

Tea light on metal jacket

1. On self-healing mat, measure, mark, and cut 5$^1/_2$-inch-by-10-inch rectangle from each sheet of paper, using ruler, pencil, and X-Acto knife.

2. Lay rectangles in horizontal orientation, overlapping adjacent short sides by $^1/_2$ inch. Use thin coat of white glue to adhere overlap.

3. Use pencil and ruler to lightly mark parallel lines, each spaced $^3/_4$ inch apart, running from top to bottom edge of vellum.

4. To make one pleat, lay length of paper in vertical orientation. Fold paper along first marked line, bringing bottom edge up to meet second marked line. Crease fold. Turn paper over and bring up fold to meet next marked line. Crease paper along fold. Continue folding paper as before until entire length of vellum is pleated.

5. Shape pleated vellum into cylinder, overlapping and gluing one pleat at each end.

6. Slip pleated cylinder around glass.

7. Place lit tea light in bottom of glass.

Embossed Monogram

An embossed monogram is an expected accent for fine linen, silver, and glassware, but it is also the perfect finish for fine candles. Using just a metal stamp with a single letter of the alphabet, you can signify your family name and decorate your candles in a minimal but sophisticated way. Metal stamps are easy to find in most stationery stores. They can also be found in antique shops where printer's typesetting blocks are sold.

YOU WILL NEED:

4-inch-square pillar candle, 4 inches high,
    in green, or in color as desired

Small saucepan

Rubber gloves

Metal stamp with letter of alphabet, or
    with motif as desired

Cotton cloth

1. Lay candle flat on clean, flat work surface.

2. Add water to pan and bring to a boil.

3. Put on gloves and pick up metal stamp by handle.

4. Carefully submerge motif end of stamp in water, heating metal for 30 seconds. Turn off heat.

5. Use cloth to wipe water off stamp, then position and press metal stamp into side of candle, using firm pressure to emboss wax. Lift off stamp and let wax cool.

Glitter Apple

Any molded candle can sparkle and shine when coated with diamond dust. These extra-fine, tiny shards of glass are made especially for applying to candles. When this sparkly dust is applied to the surface of wax fruit, candles become as enchanting and whimsical as sugarplum fairies.

YOU WILL NEED:

4 tablespoons diamond dust

Wide glass bowl

Apple-shaped candle, 3 inches high

Kraft paper

Gloves

Spray adhesive

Waxed paper

CAUTION: Handle diamond dust with care; it is made with tiny, sharp splinters of real glass.

1. Pour diamond dust into bowl and set aside.

2. Place candle on clean, flat work surface covered with Kraft paper. While wearing gloves, spray a light coat of adhesive on all surfaces of candle. Wait 5 minutes or until glue is tacky.

3. Roll candle in diamond dust until completely coated. Set candle on piece of waxed paper and allow to dry.

Bay Leaf Collar

Often the most beautiful candles are those that have the most minimal accent. Here, fragrant bay leaves are arranged in a collar around the exterior of a low, wide pillar candle. The soft, snowy white wax highlights the rich, verdant patina of the fresh leaves. Other suitable foliage is magnolia and birch leaves.

YOU WILL NEED:

20 to 25 fresh bay leaves, or other

leaves as desired

3-inch-diameter round candle,

3 inches high, in white

40 straight pins

½ yard twine in natural color

CAUTION: Remove leaves and twine

before burning candle.

1. Lay fresh leaves on flat work surface, arranging each in vertical orientation.

2. Place candle on work surface. Lay one leaf on center front of candle, tacking with pin.

3. Arrange next two leaves at either side of center leaf, slightly overlapping adjacent leaves, tacking with pins.

4. Continue as in step 3, arranging and pinning leaves around candle until leaves overlap at back.

5. Wrap twine around leaves on candle, bringing ends around to front leaf.

6. Tie twine into bow or knot. Remove pins.

Gold Stripes

A block candle can be given an elegant and glowing patina of gold in moments, transforming an ordinary pillar of wax into lighting worthy of a cathedral. Ordinary masking tape is all you need to create this strong graphic pattern. Lay two lengths of masking tape vertically on the front of the candle, and fill in the space with gold leaf.

$1\frac{1}{2}$-inch-wide masking tape

Ruler

Scissors

4-inch square multi-wick candle,

   6 inches high, in ivory or

   color as desired

Paintbrush

High-tack glue

6 sheets composition gold leaf, each

   5 inches square

Pencil with eraser

Paper towel

1. Pull off, measure, and cut eight 6-inch lengths of tape from roll, using ruler and scissors; set the tape lengths aside. To mask off a band on one face of the candle, center and attach two vertical parallel lengths of tape, allowing $1\frac{1}{2}$ inches between strips; use fingernail to press down edges of tape, pressing down ends of tape at top and bottom of candle.

2. Repeat step 1 on remaining three faces of candle.

3. Stand candle upright on flat surface. On the top of candle, apply one length of tape to each side, aligning edge of tape with edge of candle. Do not allow tape to overlap onto side.

4. Use paintbrush to apply thin coat of glue between strips of tape on one face of the candle. If glue beads, brush glued surface again until glue adheres. Wait 10 seconds or until glue becomes tacky.

5. To gild a band, tear off and attach a small piece of gold leaf to one corner of glued area between strips, tamping down gold leaf using the eraser end of a pencil. Continue to tear off and tamp down pieces of gold leaf until entire area between strips of tape is concealed. To insure a straight, clean line of gold leaf on both sides of stripe, press down edge of tape using your fingernail; then, press a flat paper towel against the gilded surface to adhere leaf. Do not rub gold leaf.

6. Repeat steps 4 and 5 on remaining three faces of candle.

7. Let glue dry 1 hour, then carefully remove strips of tape. Avoid handling gilded surfaces.

Wire Mesh Lantern

The appeal of this contemporary candle lantern is that you can make one to enclose a candle of any size. The wire mesh is fine textured and flexible. Simply cut a rectangle, fold it into a paper-bag shape, and set a pillar candle inside. While the texture of the wire mesh allows an overall glow when a pillar candle is lit, the lantern also provides an effective windscreen should you use your candle outdoors.

YOU WILL NEED:

Heavy work gloves

Fine-gauge wire mesh in aluminum

Ruler

Scissors

Pattern (page 107)

Pencil

Hot-glue gun and glue sticks

Votive candle in white

Note: Lantern cannot be used to carry candle. Position lantern first, then place candle inside.

1. While wearing gloves, measure and cut an 18$\frac{1}{2}$-inch-by-9$\frac{1}{2}$-inch rectangle from wire mesh, using ruler and scissors.

2. Lay rectangle in horizontal orientation on flat work surface.

3. Use pattern as guide to measure and lightly mark four parallel lines, each perpendicular to top edge of mesh, using ruler and pencil, as follows: one at 4$\frac{1}{2}$ inches, a second at 9 inches, a third at 13$\frac{1}{2}$ inches, and a fourth at 18 inches. You will have $\frac{1}{2}$ inch extra for overlap.

4. To make top hem, fold over $\frac{1}{2}$ inch of mesh, using edge of ruler to guide fold; press down and squeeze mesh to crease.

5. To prepare base of lantern, measure and lightly mark horizontal line across mesh, 3 inches from bottom edge.

6. Using scissors, make 3-inch-long vertical cuts in bottom hem along marked lines drawn in step 3, beginning each cut at bottom edge.

7. To cut side overlap, make $\frac{1}{2}$-inch-long horizontal cut into fold line drawn in step 5 at right edge, 3 inches from bottom, then remove section completely.

8. To fold overlap, lay ruler along marked vertical line closest to right edge of rectangle.

9. Fold overlap and press against ruler to crease.

10. Continue creasing mesh along remaining marked vertical lines as in steps 8 and 9.

11. Lay mesh rectangle on flat surface, with creases in V shape.

12. Fold up one flap and crease mesh along marked line. Fold up and crease flap at opposite side.

13. Repeat step 12 to fold remaining flaps, using dab of hot glue to secure base.

14. To finish, slide overlap to inside of lantern, using dabs of hot glue to secure.

15. Place candle inside lantern to display.

Floating Roses

If you are looking for the perfect centerpiece that is easy and elegant, search no further. Few things are as romantic as fresh flowers floating on a sparkling, clear pond. When the pond is a cut-crystal bowl filled with water, and the flowers are full-blown roses illuminated by the glow of tea lights hidden within their petals, elegance is near-guaranteed.

YOU WILL NEED:

Crystal punch bowl or other container,
 as desired

1 package plant food, such as Floralife

Spoon

3 full-blown roses in pink, or
 in color as desired

Cutting board

Sharp knife

3 tea lights in metal jackets

1. Start with clean, dry punch bowl. Fill with tepid water and add package of plant food, stirring solution with spoon.

2. To prepare flowers, lay stem of one rose on cutting board, allowing head to hang over edge of board. Use sharp knife to cut between top of stem and beginning of flower head. Repeat with remaining roses.

3. Gently separate petals of one rose until shallow cavity is created at center of bloom. Set in one tea light. Repeat process for remaining roses.

4. Place rose candles on surface of water in bowl. Light wicks when ready to use.

Moths to a Flame

These beaded bugs in hard-candy colors are the perfect guests at an outdoor summer party. They are so beautiful, you won't mind bringing them indoors when the sun goes down.

YOU WILL NEED:

2 2/3 yards (8 feet) beading wire in gold

Ruler

Scissors

Glass beads to make 8 bugs:

16 leaf beads in green;

24 round beads, each 1/8 inch in
diameter, in aqua; and

8 round beads, each 1/4 inch in
diameter, in aqua

4-inch-diameter round candle,
5 inches high

8 straight pins

Thimble

1. Measure and cut 12-inch length of wire, using ruler and scissors. Thread wire through one leaf and one 1/8-inch-diameter bead, leaving 1-inch tail. Reinsert long end of wire back into leaf, skipping 1/8-inch bead, then twist wires twice at base of leaf to secure (diagram 1).

2. Thread long end of wire into second leaf and second 1/8-inch bead. Reinsert end of wire back into leaf, skipping 1/8-inch bead, twisting wires twice at base of leaf to secure (diagram 2).

3. Thread long and short ends of wire through 1/4-inch bead and last 1/8-inch bead (diagram 3a). Then, reinsert only long end of wire back through 1/4-inch bead, skipping 1/8-inch bead (diagram 3b). Twist wire at base. Reinsert same end back through 1/4-inch and 1/8-inch bead to make antennae; leave 1 inch of wire, and cut off excess (diagram 3c).

4. Repeat steps 1 to 3 for remaining 7 bugs.

5. Position one bug on outside of candle in position as shown in photograph. Press pin into candle through twisted wires at center of wings. Use thimble if necessary.

6. Repeat step 5 for remaining 7 bugs.

7. As necessary, remove bugs as candle burns down.

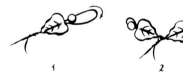

1

2

3a

3b

3c

3

glazed

Mosaic Tile

Imagine the exquisite mosaic art of Pompeii decorating your candles. This decorating method is as easy as cutting out squares of colored paper and affixing them in patterns to the side of a candle. The texture of actual tile is achieved by coating the paper with a thin layer of wax in a process called glazing.

Scissors

Paper in colors to match photograph
  or as desired

3-inch square candle, 6 inches high
  in ivory or color as desired

High-tack white glue

Double boiler

2 corncob holders

$3/4$ pound paraffin wax,
  melting point 139°F

Candy thermometer

Aluminum roasting pan

Rubber gloves

Paring knife

1. Use scissors to cut $1/4$-inch square "tiles" from paper in colors as desired.

2. Beginning at base of one side of candle, attach paper tile to left edge of candle, using dab of high-tack glue to secure; continue gluing colored tiles to candle, in approximate positions indicated in photograph, until pattern is completed.

3. To glaze candle, boil water in bottom half of double boiler.

4. Dip metal ends of corncob holders into boiling water. Insert one into top end of candle around wick, and other into bottom end. Lay candle on its side.

5. Lower heat and place top half of double boiler over boiling water. Place paraffin wax into pot and heat until melted.

6. When wax reaches 180°F on candy thermometer, turn off heat and carefully pour wax into aluminum roasting pan.

7. While wearing rubber gloves, hold candle by corncob holders, and roll candle in wax toward you in one continuous motion, skimming surface of wax until entire candle is covered. Hold upright for 15 to 30 seconds while wax hardens.

8. Repeat step 7 once or twice. Wax will lighten color of paper; do not overdip.

9. Remove corncob holders. Remove any drips at bottom of candle using paring knife. Let wax cool for 5 minutes.

Baby Shower

Rubber stamps come in such a glorious array of motifs; you will have no trouble creating a special theme candle. Here, colorful stamps decorate this candle, making a perfect gift for a new mom. First, images are stamped on a sheet of tissue paper. Then, the sheet of paper is wrapped around and affixed to the candle with the use of a heat gun.

YOU WILL NEED:

Tissue paper in white

Ruler

Pencil

Scissors

Rubber stamps: baby bottles,
    rattles, storks, cute ducks,
    and baby bunnies

Stamp pads in colors as desired

4-inch-diameter round candle,
    6 inches high, in white

10 straight pins

Heat gun

1. On clean, flat work surface, measure, mark, and cut a 9½-inch-by-6-inch rectangle from tissue paper, using ruler, pencil, and scissors.

2. Press rubber stamp in pad in desired color; press stamp down on tissue in desired position. Re-ink stamp and press down on tissue, repeating to decorate paper in random pattern or as desired. (Leave room for other stamps.)

3. Repeat step 2 using other stamps, using different color ink for each stamp.

4. When you are satisfied with design, wrap tissue paper around candle, ink side facing out. Make certain paper is flush against wax, with long edges even with top and bottom of candle; overlap paper ½ inch where ends meet. Secure top and bottom of seam with pins gently inserted into wax, just far enough to hold paper in place.

5. Carefully wave heat gun over area of paper. Wax will melt, saturate paper, and adhere to candle.

6. Repeat step 5 on all areas of candle. Remove pins.

Portrait

Now you can celebrate any occasion that is significant in the life of your family and friends by personalizing pillar candles in their honor. Simply made by gluing a photocopy of a favorite photograph to the front of a candle, the sentimental memento is then dipped in a bath of melted wax to preserve the memories you've captured.

YOU WILL NEED:

Photograph

4-inch-square candle, 6 inches high,

   in white or color as desired

Self-healing mat

Straightedge

X-Acto knife

High-tack white glue

Double boiler

2 corncob holders

$^{3}/_{4}$ pound paraffin wax, melting

   point 139°F

Candy thermometer

Aluminum roasting pan

Rubber gloves

Paring knife

Note: You will need access to a black-

   and-white photocopy machine.

1. Bring photograph and candle to copy store. Set copier on darker setting than original and make photocopy of photograph. Enlarge or reduce image to an approximately 2$^{1}/_{2}$-inch-by-3-inch rectangle or as desired.

2. On self-healing mat, trim around image using straightedge and X-Acto knife.

3. Center image and attach it to front of candle, using light dabs of glue at each corner to secure. Let glue dry.

4. Boil water in bottom half of double boiler.

5. Dip metal ends of corncob holders into boiling water. Insert one into top end of candle around wick, and other into bottom end. Lay candle on its side.

6. Lower heat and place top half of double boiler over boiling water. Place paraffin wax into pot and heat until melted.

7. When wax reaches 180°F on candy thermometer, turn off heat and carefully pour wax into aluminum roasting pan.

8. While wearing rubber gloves, hold candle by corncob holders, and roll candle in wax toward you in one continuous motion, skimming surface of wax until entire candle is covered. Hold upright for 15 to 30 seconds.

9. Repeat step 8 once or twice. Wax will lighten image; do not overdip. Remove corncob holders and stand candle upright.

10. Remove any drips at bottom of candle using paring knife. Let wax cool for 5 minutes.

Wildflowers

Pressed flowers are beautiful and colorful decorations that add country style to any candle. Varieties with small, flat petals generally work best. Gather flowers you find in your own backyard. Violets, pansies, daisies, and small leaves can be pressed the old-fashioned way, between the pages of a book, or they can be treated to a pressing in a Microfleur, a flower press made especially for a microwave oven.

YOU WILL NEED:

15 to 20 pressed flowers

4-inch-diameter round candle,
    4 inches high, in white

Double boiler

Stainless steel spoon

2 corncob holders

Dishcloth

3/4 pound paraffin wax, melting
    point 139°F

Candy thermometer

Aluminum roasting pan

Rubber gloves

Paring knife

1. Lay out pressed flowers and place candle on its side on clean, flat work surface.

2. To attach flowers to candle, boil water in bottom half of double boiler.

3. Dip bowl of spoon into boiling water for 30 seconds, remove, and dry with dishcloth. Position one flower in center of side of candle facing up. Hold hot spoon on flower petals until wax melts and flower adheres to wax.

4. Repeat steps 2 and 3 until flowers are affixed to all four sides, in pattern as desired.

5. Dip metal ends of corncob holders into boiling water. Insert one into top end of candle around wick, and other into bottom end. Lay candle on its side.

6. Lower heat and place top half of double boiler over boiling water. Place paraffin wax into pot and heat until melted.

7. When wax reaches 180°F on candy thermometer, turn off heat and carefully pour wax into aluminum roasting pan.

8. While wearing rubber gloves, hold candle by corncob holders, and roll candle in wax toward you in one continuous motion, skimming surface of wax until entire candle is covered. Hold upright for 15 to 30 seconds.

9. Repeat step 8 once or twice. Wax will lighten color of flowers; do not overdip.

10. Remove corncob holders. Remove any drips at bottom of candle with paring knife. Let wax cool for 5 minutes.

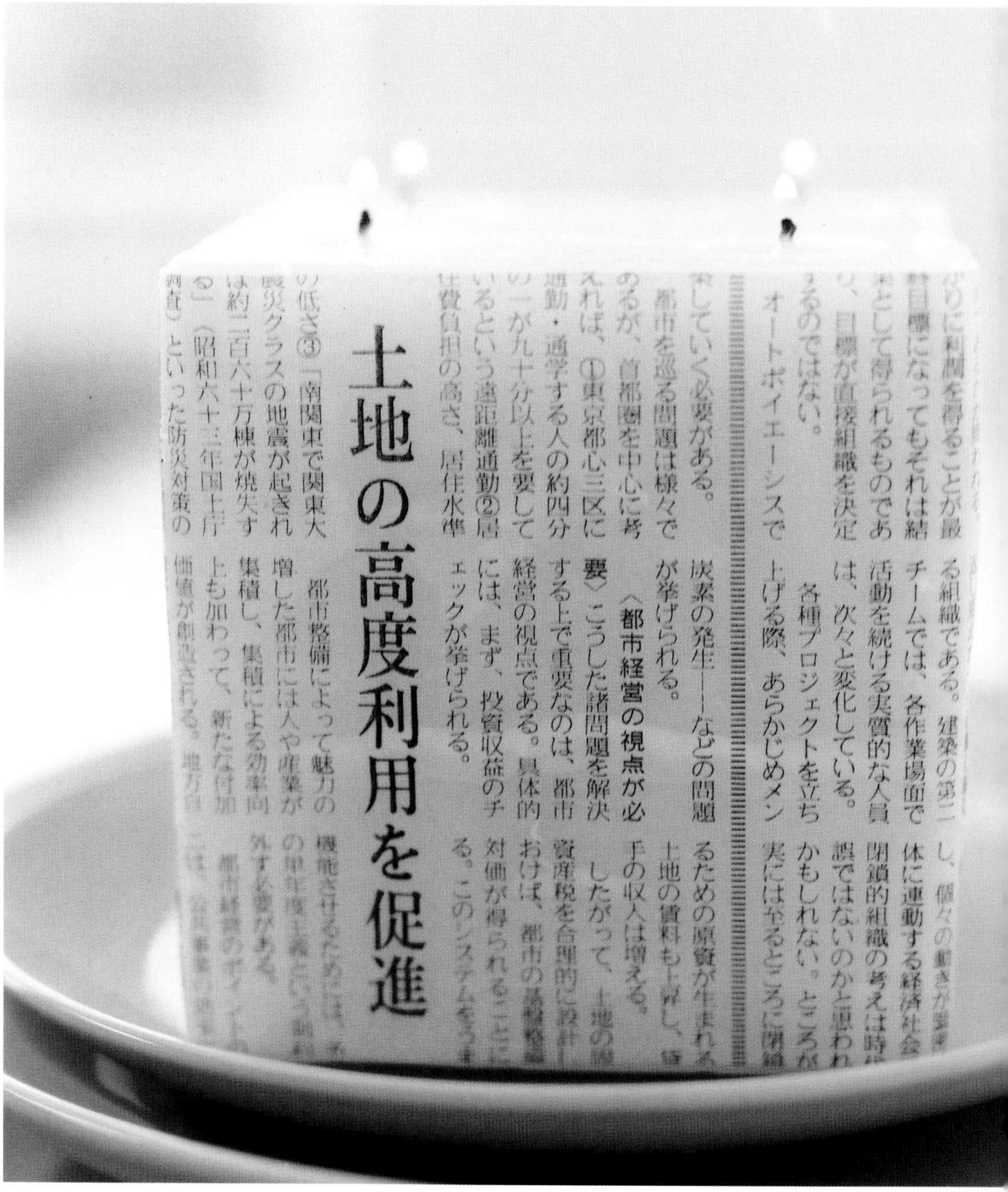
土地の高度利用を促進

Foreign Lands

Ordinary newspapers can be elevated to high art when applied to the outside of a candle. Choose a Chinese newspaper with elegantly drawn characters, or clip out single words or phrases from a French or Italian newspaper to capture the romance of these foreign locales.

YOU WILL NEED:

Foreign-language newspaper

Scissors

Cellophane tape

11-inch-by-17-inch sheet plain

   paper in white

Self-healing mat

Ruler

Pencil

X-Acto knife

4-inch square multi-wick candle,

   6 inches high, in white

2 straight pins

Heat gun

Note: You will need access to a black-

   and-white photocopy machine.

1. To make a 17-inch-by-6-inch sheet of foreign text, choose a sheet from foreign-language newspaper. If newspaper is too narrow, harvest enough text from sections as follows: Cut away blank center gutter between pages, using scissors; lay two sections on flat surface, wrong-side facing up and cut-edges aligned. Use long strip of tape to join edges. Finished page, with no break in text, should be at least 17 inches by 6 inches.

2. Photocopy finished newspaper page on 11-inch-by-17-inch plain white paper.

3. On self-healing mat, measure, mark, and cut a 16 $\frac{1}{2}$-inch-by-6-inch rectangle from copied page, using ruler, pencil, and X-Acto knife.

4. When you are satisfied with design, wrap paper around candle, with print facing out and upright. Make certain paper is flush against wax, with long edges even with top and bottom of candle; overlap paper $\frac{1}{2}$ inch where ends meet. Secure top and bottom of seam with pins gently inserted into wax, just far enough to hold paper in place.

5. Carefully wave heat gun over side of candle. Wax will melt, saturate paper, and adhere to candle. Wax cools immediately.

6. Repeat step 5 on remaining sides of candle. Remove pins.

dipped and layered

Traditional Taper

Perhaps the most traditional of all candles are dipped candles. This style of candle has a tapered shape that is formed by bathing a wick in successive layers of melted wax until a rigid candle develops. The dipping technique is an ancient one that takes time (about 1½ hours) to do, but it is one of the simplest and most straightforward. Although you can prime the wick in wax melted in the top half of a double boiler, this project calls for a dipping can, which can serve the same purpose.

15-inch length of square braid wicking for

   candle up to 2 inches in diameter

Ruler

Scissors

14-inch-high metal dipping can

Double boiler

6 $\frac{1}{2}$ pounds paraffin wax,

   melting point 145°F

Candy thermometer

Tongs

Cookie sheet

Waxed paper

Metal washer

18-inch Dowel

1 tablet wax dye (or more or less to

   achieve desired shade) in blue, or

   color as desired

Wooden spoon

Rubber gloves

3-inch-wide metal spatula

Note: If your dipping can is deep and wide,

   you can make more than one taper at a

   time. Tie the free ends of two weighted,

   primed wicks on a pencil and submerge

   them simultaneously. The level of wax

   will determine the height of the candle.

1. Measure and cut a 15-inch length of wick, using ruler and scissors.

2. To prime wick, place dipping can in bottom half of double boiler. Add paraffin wax to can. Add water to pot until it reaches halfway up dipping can. Boil water, then bring to a simmer. Heat the wax to a constant 160°F on candy thermometer until it melts. Soak wick in melted wax for 5 minutes. Use tongs to remove wick and let dry on cookie sheet covered with waxed paper. Set wick aside until wax is hard.

3. Thread one end of primed wick into washer. Tie end of wick with double knot, as close to bottom as possible, to secure washer to bottom of wick. Tie raw, opposite end to center of dowel. Dowel can be placed across the backs of two chairs set a foot apart for wax to dry.

4. Add wax dye to melted wax. Stir until blended using spoon.

5. Put on rubber gloves. Hold dowel with wick over dipping can. Lower washer end of wick into melted wax until washer touches bottom of dipping can. Submerge 3 to 4 seconds. Lift wick out of dipping can and pull wick taut for a few seconds to straighten it. Allow wax to harden.

6. Repeat process of dipping wick 10 to 30 times or until desired thickness is reached. Make certain each layer of wax hardens completely before submerging wick again.

7. To give candle smooth, even finish, heat wax to 180°F. Dip taper 3 more times, allowing wax to harden after each submersion. Turn off heat.

8. Cut wick to remove dowel and washer, using scissors. To flatten and smooth bottom end of candle, heat flat side of spatula over burner and rest uneven bottom-end on blade; allow enough wax to melt off to produce a flat bottom. Trim wick to $\frac{1}{2}$ inch, using scissors. Allow candle to set for 1 hour before using.

Over-Dipped

You can achieve the sophisticated look of a hand-dipped candle using a ready-made candle as a core. Instead of starting from scratch, dipping a naked wick in wax to build up layers, dip a purchased candle by hand. Then, form graduated layers of color by submerging the candle three-quarters of its length in the wax, then half of its length, and finally only the bottom quarter. The candle will have rings of color in subtle variations.

Dipping can, 14 inches high

Double boiler

6 $\frac{1}{2}$ pounds paraffin wax, melting point 145°F

Candy thermometer

1 tablet wax dye (or more or less to achieve desired shade) in blue, orange, purple, or colors as desired

Wooden spoon

Rubber gloves

10-inch taper candle

3-inch-wide metal spatula

Scissors

1. Place dipping can in bottom half of double boiler. Add paraffin wax to can. Add water to pot until it reaches halfway up dipping can. Boil water, then bring to a simmer. Heat until wax reaches 180°F on candy thermometer.

2. Add wax dye to paraffin wax. Stir until blended, using wooden spoon. Wax should be almost to top of dipping can.

3. Put on rubber gloves. Hold candle by wick and lower into the wax until completely covered. Submerge for 3 to 4 seconds. Lift candle out of dipping can by wick and allow wax to harden.

4. Repeat step 3 two more times, first dipping only three-quarters of the way up the candle and then just one-half, and finally one-quarter, thus creating rings of graduated color. Make certain each layer of wax hardens completely before submerging candle again. Turn off heat.

5. To flatten and smooth bottom end of candle, heat flat side of spatula over burner and rest uneven bottom-end on blade; allow enough wax to melt off to produce a flat bottom. Trim wick to $\frac{1}{2}$ inch, using scissors. Allow candle to set for 1 hour before using.

Snowball

You can almost see the cold mist rising from this witty replica of a frosty snowball. The snowball candle is also one of the easiest and most fun you will have occasion to make. All you do is add a coat of high-grade whipped wax to the exterior of a purchased globe-shaped candle.

YOU WILL NEED:

Double boiler

$^3/_4$ ounce stearin

$^1/_2$ pound paraffin wax,
  melting point 145°F

Wooden spoon

Candy thermometer

Glass mixing bowl

Eggbeater

3-inch-diameter globe-shaped
  candle in white

Aluminum foil

Rubber gloves

Stainless-steel spoon

Butter knife (optional)

1. Boil water in bottom half of double boiler.

2. Melt stearin and paraffin wax together in top half of double boiler. Stir until blended, using wooden spoon. Heat until mixture reaches about 185°F on candy thermometer. Do not let wax get hotter than 200°F.

3. When mixture reaches desired temperature, turn off heat and transfer hot wax to glass mixing bowl. Allow to cool until a fine, foamy skin develops on surface.

4. Whip wax using eggbeater until foamy lather forms.

5. Place candle on work surface covered with aluminum foil.

6. Put on rubber gloves. Spoon whipped wax on entire surface of candle, without concealing the wick. Rotate candle for even coverage. When complete, set decorated candle on foil. While wax is still soft, use knife to create more texture if desired.

Gift Bundle

One of the easiest ways to make your own candles is to roll them! All you need is beeswax and wicks. Beeswax comes in large sheets and in tropical colors. Simply roll up a sheet of wax, trapping a wick inside. Make a few fat candles in different colors, then gather them in a little bundle and tie them with a pretty ribbon for the perfect hostess gift.

YOU WILL NEED:

Ruler

Scissors

3 3/4-foot (45 inches) length primed
   24-ply flat braid wick for candles 1 to
   2 inches in diameter (see instructions
   for priming wicks on page 61)

Waxed paper

5 sheets of honeycomb beeswax,
   each 8 inches by 16 1/2 inches, in
   natural, lavendar, pale blue, and
   yellow, or color as desired

Hair dryer

1/2 yard ribbon, 1 inch wide

1. Using ruler and scissors, measure and cut wick into five 9-inch lengths. Set aside.

2. Cover clean, flat work surface with waxed paper. Lay one sheet of beeswax on waxed paper in horizontal orientation. Using hair dryer, warm wax until malleable.

3. Lay wick parallel to left-hand edge of beeswax sheet, allowing top end of wick to extend 1 inch beyond top edge of sheet and keeping bottom end of wick flush with bottom edge of sheet. Use hands to roll edge of wax against wick, pressing wax to trap wick securely.

4. Continue to roll wax in even rod shape until all wax is used. If necessary, warm final edge of wax, using hair dryer set on warm, then gently press full length of edge to candle to secure. Trim wick to 1/2 inch, using scissors.

5. Repeat steps 2 through 4 with remaining 4 sheets of beeswax.

6. Bundle candles together and tie with ribbon, finishing with a bow in front.

Stacked Star

It you have ever made cookies using a cookie cutter, this bright candle will be a snap. All you do is cut out star shapes from sheets of beeswax using a cookie cutter. Then, you pile the stars in a little stack, add a primed wick, and presto: a twinkling star for your table or anywhere you want a little starlight.

YOU WILL NEED:

Waxed paper

2 sheets of flat beeswax, each 8 inches
    by 16 1/2 inches, in gold, or color as
    desired

Hair dryer

1 1/2 inch metal cookie cutter in
    star shape

Soup can

Pencil with eraser

Votive wick pin

Scissors

10-inch primed papercore wick
    (see instructions for priming
    wicks on page 61)

Wick tab

1. Cover clean, flat work surface with waxed paper. Lay one sheet of beeswax on work surface.

2. Using hair dryer, warm wax until malleable.

3. Position cookie cutter on wax. Place soup can over cookie cutter and press down. This will protect your hands and ensure even pressure. Lift up cookie cutter and gently nudge star out using pencil eraser, being careful to avoid distorting shape of star. Set star aside.

4. Continue to cut stars from wax, repeating step 3, until desired number is achieved (about 60).

5. Lay one star on clean, flat work surface. Place another star on top keeping edges even. Continue adding more stars until desired height of candle is reached.

6. Carefully poke hole straight down through center of stack, using wick pin.

7. Cut wick, using scissors (about 2 or 3 inches longer than height of stack). Attach one end of wick to wick tab. Thread opposite end of wick through hole at bottom of stack, through center of stack and out top opening. Slide stars down wick to avoid open spaces between them. Trim wick to 1/2 inch.

Wax Fruit

You can decorate the sides of a large block candle with ripe-looking fruit, each piece seeming luscious enough to eat. Each piece of fruit is actually made by using a cookie cutter pressed into a layer of smooth, colorful beeswax. (The wax is so pliable it can be applied to a candle simply by pressing it on!) Near-instant to decorate, this candle makes a sumptuous centerpiece for entertaining.

YOU WILL NEED:

Waxed paper

Sheets of flat beeswax, each 8 inches by
   16$\frac{1}{2}$ inches, in green, red, purple,
   apricot, gold, or colors as desired

Hair dryer

Fruit-shaped cookie cutters: apple,
   cherries, grapes, pineapple, leaves,
   or shapes as desired

Soup can

Pencil with eraser

Paring knife

4-inch square multi-wick candle, 6 inches
   high, in white or ivory (each face must
   be at least $\frac{1}{2}$ inch larger all around
   than width of cutters)

Designer's Tip: If a grape-shaped cookie
cutter is unavailable, use a leaf shape and
a small round cookie cutter.

1. Cover clean, flat work surface with waxed paper. Lay sheet of beeswax on work surface. (Use green for apple, red for cherries, etc.)

2. Using hair dryer, warm wax until malleable.

3. Position cookie cutter on wax. Place soup can over cookie cutter and press down. This will protect your hands and ensure even pressure. Lift up cookie cutter and gently nudge fruit shape out using pencil eraser, being careful to avoid distorting shape of fruit. Set fruit-shaped wax aside.

4. Repeat steps 1 through 3 to press and cut out one bunch of grapes, one pineapple, leaves, with motif of each cookie cutter corresponding to appropriate color of wax; lay wax fruit on flat, waxed-paper-covered surface.

5. Use paring knife to inscribe extra details on surface of fruit or leaves, as desired, making certain not to cut all the way through wax.

6. To decorate one face of candle, lay candle flat on work surface. Press one piece of wax fruit onto center of candle face. If wax fruit does not stick to candle wax, warm fruit shape using hair dryer set on warm, then press fruit shape onto candle face.

7. Repeat step 6 to decorate remaining three faces of candle, using one piece of wax fruit per face.

Puzzle Cubes

Now you can put two candles together as you would a kid's puzzle. Simply stack and tack two candles of contrasting colors together, and insert a new wick through both. When you dip the colorful combo into a wax bath, two candles become one pretty cube. Burnish the wax surface with a nylon stocking (!) to polish the duo to a super shine.

4 square votive candles, each 2 inches

   wide by 2 inches high: 2 in gold

   and 2 in cranberry, or colors as desired

Paring knife

Tweezers

8 straight beading pins, each $1/2$ inch long

   (or straight pins cut to $1/2$ inch using

   wire cutters)

Small, lightweight hammer

Saucepan

Rubber gloves

6-inch-length galvanized wire,

   medium gauge (or any wire that

   will not enlarge the wick hole)

Dishcloth

2 precut primed wicks, each 4 inches long

   (see instructions for priming

   wicks on page 61)

2 wick tabs

Cookie sheet

Waxed paper

Double boiler

1 pound paraffin wax,

   melting point 129°F

Candy thermometer

Nylon stockings

Scissors

1. Remove wicks from all four candles, using paring knife to pry up tab, and tweezers to pull tab and wick out through bottom of candle.

2. Lay one candle on clean, flat work surface, tab hole facing up. Insert head of pin into each corner of candle, $1/4$ inch from edge, using gentle taps of hammer to drive pins halfway into wax. Position second candle on first, wick hole facing down, and press on top candle to join.

3. Repeat step 2 with remaining candles.

4. Fill saucepan with water and bring to boil. Put on rubber gloves. Dip galvanized wire in boiling water, wipe dry with dishcloth, and insert end through wick hole in top candle of each stack. Remove wire.

5. Attach one precut primed wick to wick tab by trapping one end of wick in jaws of tab. Insert opposite end of wick into hole at bottom of one candle stack, pushing wick up through top hole and allowing wick tab to rest on bottom of stack.

6. Repeat step 5 with second stack of candles.

7. Cover cookie sheet with waxed paper. Set aside.

8. Boil water in bottom half of double boiler. Melt paraffin wax in top half of double boiler until it reaches 150°F on candy thermometer. Wearing gloves, hold one candle stack by wick and lower into wax, coating all sides. Lift candle stack out of wax and set on cookie sheet to cool.

9. Repeat step 8 with remaining stack.

10. Burnish candle using nylon stockings that have been balled up, using circular motion to smooth and shine all surfaces. Trim wicks to $1/2$ inch, using scissors.

poured

China Cup

The conviviality of afternoon tea is enhanced when the table is illuminated by the glow of a candle housed in a delicately patterned china cup made of the finest English porcelain. Here, a flea-market find, with a few imperfections, is transformed into a charming lighting accent for the table. And after the candle has burned down, simply run the cup under hot water and use a knife to pop out the remaining candle stub. Use the tea cup again for another candle or simply as a decorative accent in your home.

(see instructions for priming wicks on page 61)

YOU WILL NEED:

4 inches of primed papercore wick

(see instructions for priming wicks

on page 61)

Wick tab

China cup

Mold sealer

Chopstick

Double boiler

1 tablet wax dye (or more or less to

achieve desired shade) to match

china, or in color as desired

$1/2$ pound paraffin wax,

melting point 129°F

Wooden spoon

Candy thermometer

Oven mitt

Ladle with lip

Skewer

Scissors

1. Trap one end of wick in jaws of wick tab. Place wick tab in bottom of cup, securing it with mold sealer. Tie opposite end of wick to center of chopstick, laying chopstick across top of cup. Set cup aside.

2. Boil water in bottom half of double boiler. Melt wax dye and paraffin wax together in top half of double boiler. Stir until blended, using wooden spoon. Heat until mixture reaches about 150°F on candy thermometer. Do not let wax get hotter than 180°F.

3. When mixture reaches desired temperature, turn off heat. Put on oven mitt to hold cup while pouring wax. Cup will get hot. Tilt cup and use ladle to pour wax into cup onto interior wall, then stand cup upright until wax is $1/8$ inch from rim. Let wax cool 1 hour. Wax will shrink, forming well near wick. Poke hole in wax skin using skewer, and fill well with melted wax. Let cool. Repeat process, as necessary.

4. Let candle set 3 to 4 hours or overnight.

5. Untie wick from chopstick. Trim top wick to $1/2$ inch using scissors.

Miniature Paint Can

For a great housewarming gift, consider making a trio of these candles housed in miniature paint cans. You can buy brand-new cans in an art-supply store. Then the fun begins. Make several batches of wax, each in a color that matches the band of gift wrap that encircles the can. Tie a ribbon around each can, and attach a color-coordinated gift tag.

Scrap paper for template

3-inch-diameter paint tin

Tape measure

Scissors

Patterned gift wrap

Self-healing mat

Ruler

Pencil

X-Acto knife

6-inch length primed papercore wick

   (see instructions for priming wicks

   on page 61)

Wick tab

Mold sealer

Chopstick

Double boiler

1 tablet wax dye (or more or less to

   achieve desired shade) to match paper

2 pounds paraffin wax,

   melting point 129°F

Wooden spoon

Candy thermometer

Oven mitt

Ladle with lip

Skewer

Kraft paper

Spray adhesive

$1/2$ yard ribbon in red

Gift tag

1. Measure and cut a rectangle of scrap paper that wraps around and covers can, adding $1/2$ inch extra for overlap at back, using tape measure and scissors. Use this as template to make band for tin from patterned gift wrap as follows: Lay gift wrap, wrong-side facing up, on self-healing mat; lay template on gift wrap. Use ruler and pencil to trace template. Use X-Acto knife to cut out. Set gift-wrap band aside.

2. Trap one end of wick in jaws of wick tab. Place wick tab in bottom of tin, securing it with mold sealer. Tie opposite end of wick to center of chopstick, laying chopstick across top of tin. Set tin aside.

3. Boil water in bottom half of double boiler. Melt wax dye and paraffin wax together in top half of double boiler. Stir until blended, using wooden spoon. Heat until mixture reaches about 150°F on candy thermometer. Do not let wax get hotter than 180°F.

4. When mixture reaches desired temperature, turn off heat. Put on oven mitt to hold can while pouring wax. Can will get hot. Tilt tin and use ladle to pour wax into tin onto interior wall, then stand tin upright and continue to pour until wax is $1/8$ inch from rim. Let wax cool 1 hour. Wax will shrink, forming well near wick. Poke hole in wax skin using skewer, and fill well with melted wax. Allow to cool. Repeat process, as necessary.

5. Let candle set 3 to 4 hours or overnight.

6. Untie wick from chopstick. Trim wick to $1/2$ inch, using scissors.

7. Cover work surface with Kraft paper. Apply light coat of spray adhesive to back of gift-wrap rectangle. Wait 5 minutes or until surface is tacky. Wrap band around tin, overlapping band in back.

8. Wrap ribbon around tin and tie bow.

CAUTION: Candles made in metal containers get hot. Do not handle tin until it cools. Be careful handling candle when lit. Keep the container away from children.

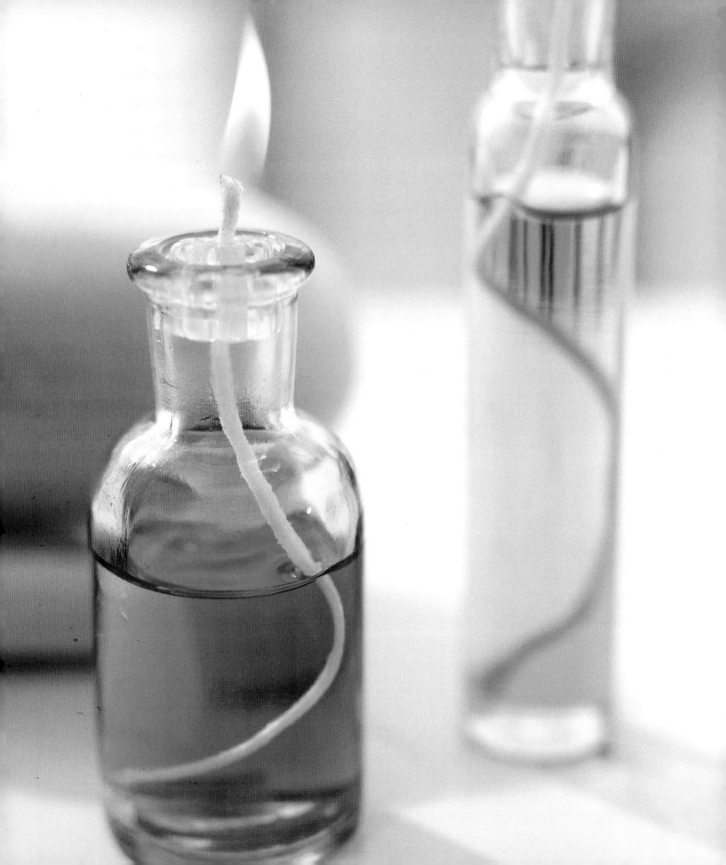

Oil Lamp

An ancient light source, oil lamps are composed, in principle, of only two elements: a container filled with oil and a wick. The unique glow of an oil lamp can be easily created using a pretty bottle, lamp oil, and a glass bead through which a wick is threaded. The absorption of the oil through the wick provides an almost continuous flame of illumination. Add more oil to maintain the flame.

YOU WILL NEED:

Square braid wick for container with
  2-inch-diameter neck or less

Slender 8-ounce glass bottle with
  $3/4$-inch-diameter neck opening

Scissors

8 ounces lamp oil

Chopstick

Glass bead with diameter slightly larger
  than bottle neck opening and with hole
  large enough to thread wick

1. Cut wick to length equal to height of bottle plus $1^1/_2$ inches, using scissors.

2. Pour lamp oil into bottle until oil is $1/_2$ inch from rim.

3. Prime wick by submerging in oil, using chopstick to prod full length into bottle.

4. Remove wick from bottle, pulling wick between fingers to get rid of excess oil.

5. Thread one end of wick through hole in bead, allowing end to extend past hole by 1 inch.

6. Submerge other end of wick in bottle, allowing bead to rest in neck opening.

Hanging Citrus

You can use a fresh lemon as a beautiful container for candles. Just add color, fragrance, and a ribbon hanger. These charming votives make perfect summer lighting for your porch or garden trellis! For variation, slice off a small portion of the bottom rind, just enough to create a flat bottom. Omit the beads, and wrap the ribbon horizontally around the lemon and tie a bow. Then, place a glowing lemon candle at each place setting at your next garden party!

3 fresh lemons

Cutting board

Sharp knife

Serrated spoon

Awl

3 beads

3 small papercore primed wicks, each 5

   inches long (see instructions for priming

   wicks on page 61)

3 Chopsticks

Mold sealer

Empty egg carton

Double boiler

1 tablet wax dye (or more or less to

   achieve desired shade) in yellow

$1^{1}/_{2}$ pounds paraffin wax,

   melting point 129°F

Wooden spoon

Candy thermometer

Lemon-scented oil

Oven mitt

Ladle with lip

3 lengths of double-sided satin ribbon,

   each 12 inches long, in yellow

Skewer

Scissors

1. Place one lemon on cutting board and use knife to slice off top inch of lemon; scrape out pulp using serrated spoon.

2. Poke hole in bottom of lemon using awl. Tie a bead to one end of wick, then thread opposite end in through hole in underside of lemon and tie to center of chopstick, laying chopstick across top of lemon. Seal hole on underside with dab of mold sealer. Place lemon in one compartment of egg carton, and set aside.

3. Repeat steps 1 and 2 with two remaining lemons.

4. Boil water in bottom half of double boiler.

5. Melt wax dye and paraffin wax together in top half of double boiler. Stir until blended, using wooden spoon. Heat until mixture reaches about around 150°F on candy thermometer. Do not let wax get hotter than 180°F.

6. When mixture reaches desired temperature, turn off heat. Stir in 5 drops of lemon-scented oil. Put on oven mitt to hold lemon while pouring wax. Lemon will get hot. Tilt lemon and use ladle to pour wax into lemon onto interior wall, then stand lemon upright and continue to pour until wax is $^{1}/_{8}$ inch from top.

7. To add ribbon loop, fold one length of ribbon in half and push 1 inch of each ribbon end into opposite sides of lemon along cavity wall. When wax cools, it will trap ends.

8. Let wax cool 1 hour. Wax will shrink, forming well near wick. Poke hole in wax skin using skewer, and fill well with melted wax. Allow wax to cool. Repeat process, as necessary.

9. Let candle set 3 to 4 hours or overnight. Untie wick from chopstick.

10. Trim top wick to $^{1}/_{2}$ inch, using scissors.

11. Repeat steps 6 through 10 with remaining lemons.

Seashells

The aesthetic appeal of these little tea-light candles is matched by the ease of crafting each charming lighting accent. Using only a bit of melted paraffin wax, you can transform seashells into tea lights for your table.

YOU WILL NEED:

4 clam shells, each at least $^{1}/_{2}$ inch deep

Dishwashing liquid

Paper towels

4 small papercore primed wicks, each
   3 inches long (see instructions for
   priming wicks on page 61)

4 wick tabs

Mold sealer

Double boiler

$^{1}/_{4}$ pound paraffin wax,
   melting point 129°F

Wooden spoon

Candy thermometer

Large metal spoon

Skewer

Scissors

Note: Tea-light candles will burn
approximately 20 minutes.

1. Wash shells in hot water with dishwashing liquid and dry with paper towels. Place shells in warm oven for 10 minutes to dry them completely. Remove shells from oven and place on protected work surface, with opening facing up.

2. Trap one end of wick in jaws of wick tab. Place wick tab in bottom of shell, securing it with mold sealer.

3. Repeat step 2 with remaining shells.

4. Boil water in bottom half of double boiler.

5. Melt paraffin wax in top half of double boiler, stirring occasionally, using wooden spoon, until wax reaches 150°F on candy thermometer. Do not let wax get hotter than 180°F.

6. When wax reaches desired temperature, turn off heat. Using metal spoon, carefully spoon wax into shells until wax is within $^{1}/_{8}$ inch of rim. Let wax cool 30 minutes. Wax will shrink, forming well near wicks. Poke holes in wax skin using skewer, and fill wells with melted wax. Let wax cool another 30 minutes. Repeat process, as necessary.

7. Let candles set 3 to 4 hours or overnight.

8. Trim wicks to $^{1}/_{2}$ inch, using scissors.

Mason Jar

For an interesting and fun summer-party candle, pour melted wax into recycled glassware. Here, a mason jar filled with wax gives this chunky candle charm. This is also a great project for using tumblers that have no mates.

YOU WILL NEED:

Mason jar

Glass cleaner

Paper towels

10-inch-long small primed papercore wick

   (see instructions for priming wicks

    on page 61)

Wick tab

Mold sealer

Chopstick

Double boiler

2 pounds paraffin wax,

   melting point 129°F

Candy thermometer

Oven mitt

Ladle with lip

Skewer

Scissors

1. Thoroughly clean jar, using glass cleaner and paper towels, to remove any grease or fingerprints.

2. Trap one end of wick in jaws of wick tab. Place wick tab in bottom of jar, securing it with mold sealer. Tie opposite end of wick to center of chopstick, laying chopstick across top of jar. Set jar aside.

3. Boil water in bottom half of double boiler.

4. Melt paraffin wax in top half of double boiler. Heat until mixture reaches about 150°F on candy thermometer. Do not let wax get hotter than 180°F.

5. When mixture reaches desired temperature, turn off heat. Put on oven mitt to hold jar while pouring wax. Jar will get hot. Tilt jar and ladle wax onto interior wall. Then stand jar upright and continue to pour until wax is 1/8 inch from rim. Let wax cool 1 hour. Wax will shrink, forming well near wick. Poke hole in wax skin using skewer, and fill well with melted wax. Allow to cool. Repeat process as necessary.

6. Let candle set 3 to 4 hours or overnight.

7. Untie wick from chopstick. Trim top wick to 1/2 inch, using scissors.

Salt Cellar

One of the quickest ways to make a candle is to use Candle Dust. Made from finely granulated paraffin wax, the wax dust comes in beautiful colors. Pour a mound of it into a beautiful container in which a wick has been placed, light the wick, and voilà! You've just made a votive candle in less than 5 minutes!

YOU WILL NEED:

3-inch-long small primed papercore wick

   (see instructions for priming wicks

   on page 61)

Wick tab

Salt cellar with 2-inch-diameter

   opening, $1^{1}/_{2}$ inches deep

1 ounce Candle Dust in white

1. Trap one end of wick in jaws of wick tab, and place wick tab in center bottom of salt cellar.

2. Holding wick straight, pour Candle Dust into salt cellar until dust is $^{1}/_{4}$ inch from rim.

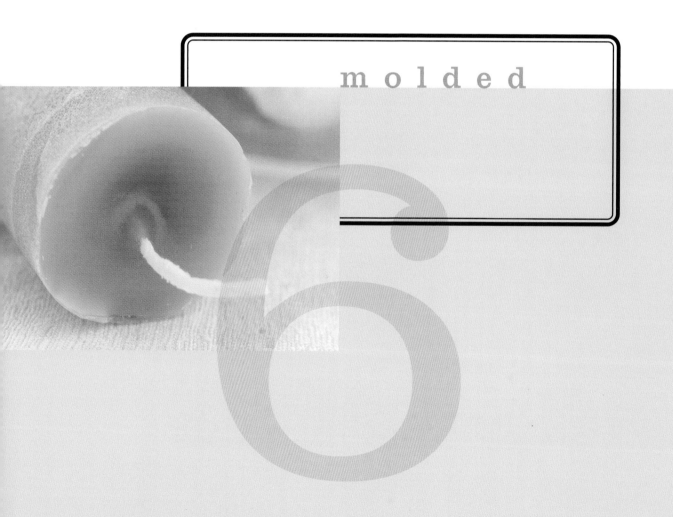

molded

6

Weathered Pillar

Create this distressed-looking candle by lining a metal mold with corrugated paper to create the textured surface. After the candle cools and is removed from the mold, you peel away the paper to reveal fluted columns around the candle.

YOU WILL NEED:

Awl

Hammer

15-ounce empty soup can,
    cleaned and dried

Nonstick cooking spray

Self-healing mat

1 large piece corrugated paper

Ruler

Pencil

X-Acto knife

Spray bottle filled with water

Dishcloth

Masking tape

6 inches of primed square braid
    wick for candle 2 to 4 inches in
    diameter (see instructions for
    priming wicks on page 61)

Metal washer

Mold sealer

Chopstick

1. Use awl and hammer to create small hole in center of bottom of soup can. Apply coat of nonstick cooking spray to inside of can. Set aside.

2. On self-healing mat, measure, mark, and cut a 10-inch-by-4$\frac{1}{4}$-inch rectangle from corrugated paper (with ridges running vertically when rectangle is wrapped around can), using ruler, pencil, and X-Acto knife.

3. To prevent paper from sticking to candle, use spray bottle filled with water to moisten paper on ridged side. Place moistened paper on dishcloth for 5 minutes, then apply coat of nonstick cooking spray to ridged side of paper.

4. Make sleeve from corrugated paper by bringing two short ends together, ridged-side of paper facing inward, and fit inside the can, using masking tape to secure overlap.

5. Tie one end of wick to washer. Thread opposite end of wick through hole in underside of can, securing washer with mold sealer. Pull opposite end of wick up through can and tie to center of chopstick, laying chopstick across top of can. Wick should be taut. Set can aside.

6. Boil water in bottom half of double boiler.

7. Melt stearin and parafin wax together in top half of double boiler. Stir until blended, using wooden spoon. Heat until mixture reaches about 180°F on candy thermometer. Do not let wax get hotter than 200°F. Stir until blended.

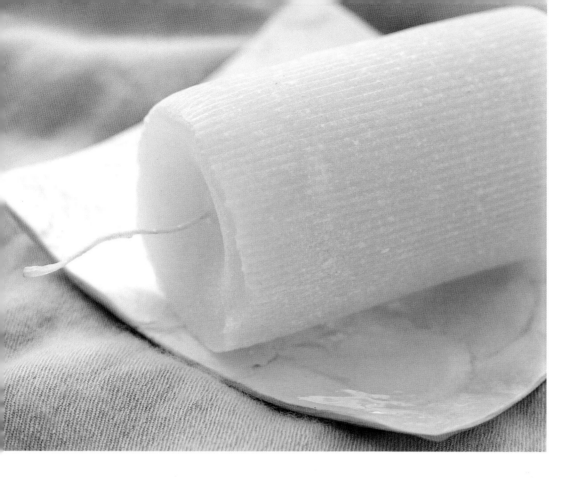

Metal washer

Mold sealer

Chopstick

Double boiler

1 1/2 ounces stearin

1 pound paraffin wax, melting point 140°F

Wooden spoon

Candy thermometer

Oven mitt

Ladle with lip

Skewer

Scissors

8. When mixture reaches desired temperature, turn off heat. Put on oven mitt to hold soup can while pouring wax. Can will get hot. Tilt can and use ladle to pour wax into can onto interior wall, then stand can upright and continue to pour until wax is 1/8 inch from rim. Let wax cool 1 hour. Wax will shrink, forming well near wick. Poke hole in wax skin using skewer, and fill well with melted wax. Let cool. Repeat process, as necessary.

9. Let candle set 3 to 4 hours or overnight.

10. Untie wick from chopstick and clip off washer from bottom of can, using scissors. Tap can on side and remove paper-wrapped candle.

11. Carefully peel paper away from candle. If paper sticks, hold under running water and rub paper to remove it.

12. Trim away excess bottom wick and trim top wick to 1/2 inch.

Faux Alabaster

The textural effect on the surface of the candle is made when the melted wax is first absorbed by the fibers of the cardboard mold into which it is poured.

YOU WILL NEED:

Awl

Round disposable plastic lid

Nonstick cooking spray

Cardboard paper-towel tube

Mold sealer

18-inch length of primed square braid wick

   for candle up to 2 inches in diameter

   (see instructions for priming wicks on

   page 61)

Metal washer

Chopstick

Double boiler

1 ounce stearin

1 tablet wax dye (or more or less to

   achieve desired shade) in red, yellow,

   or color as desired

Wooden spoon

2 pounds paraffin wax,

   melting point 140°F

Candy thermometer

Oven mitt

Ladle

Skewer

Scissors

1. Using awl, poke hole through center of clean, disposable plastic lid.

2. Apply coat of nonstick cooking spray to interior of cardboard tube. Center tube over hole in lid. Secure tube to lid by packing mold sealer around bottom edge.

3. Tie one end of wick to metal washer. Thread opposite end of wick through hole in underside of lid, securing washer with mold sealer. Tie opposite end of wick to center of chopstick, laying chopstick across top of tube. Wick should be taut. Set tube aside.

4. Boil water in bottom half of double boiler.

5. Melt stearin and wax dye together in top half of double boiler. Stir until blended, using wooden spoon. Add paraffin wax and heat until mixture reaches about 155°F on candy thermometer. Do not let wax get hotter than 165°F. Stir until blended.

6. When mixture reaches desired temperature, turn off heat. Put on oven mitt to hold tube while pouring wax. Tube will get hot. Tilt tube and use ladle to pour wax into tube onto interior wall, then stand tube upright and continue to pour until wax is $1/8$ inch from rim. Let wax cool 1 hour. Wax will shrink, forming well near wick. Poke hole in wax skin using skewer, and fill well with melted wax. Let cool. Repeat process, as necessary.

7. Let candle set 3 to 4 hours or overnight.

8. Untie wick from chopstick. Carefully peel paper away from candle. If paper sticks, hold under running water and rub paper to remove it.

9. Clip off washer and trim away excess bottom wick and trim top wick to $\frac{1}{2}$ inch, using scissors.

Alternately stand candle on its bottom and top for 2 to 3 seconds at a time in top half of double boiler over boiling water; this process will melt down wax slightly to smooth out any rough surfaces.

Eggshells

Some of the most uniquely shaped candles can be made using molds found around the house. The secret to these glowing renditions of Easter eggs is to use ordinary eggshells to make perfectly oval candles. Make up a few dozen egg candles and position them in egg cups for a brightly lit spring luncheon.

YOU WILL NEED:

Sharp knife

6 raw eggs

Chopstick

Bowl

6 primed small papercore wicks, each

    5 inches long (see instructions for

    priming wicks on page 61)

Mold sealer

Empty egg carton

Double boiler

$1/2$ pound paraffin wax,

    melting point 129°F

Wooden spoon

Candy thermometer

1 tablet white dye, or color as desired

Glass measuring cup

Skewer

Scissors

1. Use point of knife blade to tap out $1/8$-inch-wide hole in shell at narrow end of raw egg; repeat process to make $1/2$-inch-wide hole at broad end of egg. Repeat with remaining eggs.

2. Use chopstick to pierce egg membrane, then blow through smaller hole to empty egg into bowl; repeat with remaining eggs.

3. Rinse interior of shells and place eggs in warm oven for 2 hours to dry.

4. Insert one wick into wick hole at narrow end of egg, feeding all but $1/2$ inch of wick through center cavity and out through large hole; repeat process with remaining eggs.

5. Press wad of mold sealer on wick and wick hole at bottom to secure; repeat with remaining eggs.

6. Stand eggs upright in empty egg carton.

7. Boil water in bottom half of double boiler.

8. Melt paraffin wax in top half of double boiler. Stir occasionally, using wooden spoon. Heat wax until it reaches around 150°F on candy thermometer. Add wax dye to melted wax, stirring to blend. Do not let wax get hotter than 165°F.

9. Position eggs, large holes facing up, in egg carton.

10. When mixture reaches desired temperature, turn off heat. Transfer melted wax to measuring cup and pour into empty shells until wax reaches rim of large hole.

11. As wax hardens, wax will shrink, forming well near wick. Poke hole in wax skin using skewer, and fill well with melted wax. Wait 30 minutes. Repeat process, as necessary.

12. Let candles set overnight.

13. Peel off shells; glaze eggs by holding wicks and lowering them into dyed wax.

14. Stand eggs upright and let glaze dry; trim wicks, using scissors.

Potpourri

You can add aromatherapeutic benefits to your candles. Just add floral potpourri and candle fragrance, and you can customize a candle to suit your personal tastes. The potpourri adds pretty color and texture to the candle, while the fragrance can evoke fantasies of walks through a forest or a flowering garden.

Primed square braid wick for candle

    4 to 6 inches in diameter (see instruc-

    tion for priming wicks on page 61)

Metal washer

$4^1/2$-inch square candle mold,

    6 inches high

Mold sealer

Chopstick

Double boiler

$1^1/2$ ounces stearin

1 tablet wax dye (or more or less to

    achieve desired shade) in purple,

    or color as desired

Wooden spoon

2 pounds paraffin wax,

    melting point 140°F

Candy thermometer

Candle fragrance in rose, or fragrance

    as desired

$1/2$ cup potpourri (use potpourri with

    darker colors because heat will

    distort and "bleach" colors)

Nonstick cooking spray

Oven mitt

Ladle with lip

Skewer

Scissors

1. Tie one end of wick to washer. Thread opposite end of wick through hole in underside of mold, securing washer with mold sealer. Pull opposite end of wick up through mold and tie to center of chopstick, laying chopstick across top of mold. Wick should be taut. Set mold aside.

2. Boil water in bottom half of double boiler.

3. Melt stearin and wax dye in top half of double boiler. Stir until blended, using wooden spoon. Add paraffin wax and stir mixture, continuing to heat until mixture reaches about 180°F on candy thermometer. Do not let wax get hotter than 200°F.

4. When mixture reaches desired temperature, turn off heat. Stir in 5 drops of candle fragrance. Pour in potpourri and stir all ingredients until blended.

5. Apply coat of nonstick cooking spray to interior of mold. Put on oven mitt to hold mold while pouring wax. Mold will get hot. Tilt mold and use ladle to pour wax into mold onto interior wall, then stand mold upright and continue to pour until wax is $1/8$ inch from rim. Let wax cool 1 hour. Wax will shrink, forming well near wick. Poke hole in wax skin using skewer, and fill well with melted wax. Allow to cool 1 hour. Repeat process, as necessary.

6. Let candle set 3 to 4 hours or overnight.

7. Untie wick from chopstick and clip off washer from bottom of mold, using scissors. Tap on side of mold and slide candle out.

8. Trim away excess bottom wick and trim top wick to $1/2$ inch. Alternately stand candle on its bottom and top for 2 to 3 seconds at a time in top half of double boiler over boiling water; this process will melt down wax slightly to smooth out any rough surfaces.

Beach Light

Using wet sand to mold free-form candles is one of the oldest and easiest ways to create beautiful lighting accents for outdoor decorating. Next time you are at the beach, collect a few buckets of sand and use them to create a mold into which you will pour the melted wax. You will be pleasantly surprised to find that the sand will cling to cool wax and add an attractive granular texture to the exterior of the candle.

10 cups sand

Large bowl

Small fluted cake pan, 4$\frac{1}{2}$ inches
in diameter, 3 inches high

Double boiler

1$\frac{1}{2}$ ounces stearin

1 tablet wax dye (or more or less to
achieve desired shade) in blue, or
color as desired

Wooden spoon

1 pound paraffin wax, melting point 140°F

Candy thermometer

Citronella oil

Ladle with lip

Skewer

5-inch length primed square braid wick for
candle 4 to 6 inches in diameter (see
directions for priming wicks on page 61)

Chopstick

Scissors

Note: Wax will seep into the sand when
first poured, so you will need more wax
than you would for a regular mold.

1. Pour sand into large bowl, adding water $\frac{1}{4}$ cup at a time until sand holds the imprint of a fist. Use hands to scoop out well in center, leaving at least a 4-inch wall of sand on sides.

2. To make mold, push cake pan into center well, open-side facing up. Use hand to pack sand firmly in a layer around center hole of pan. Remove pan.

3. Boil water in bottom half of double boiler.

4. Melt stearin and wax dye together in top half of double boiler. Stir until blended, using wooden spoon. Add paraffin wax and heat until mixture reaches about 180°F on candy thermometer. Do not let wax get hotter than 200°F.

5. When mixture reaches desired temperature, turn off heat. Add 5 to 7 drops of citronella oil and stir until blended.

6. Use ladle to carefully pour wax into center of mold, avoiding walls of mold to prevent crumbling. As wax seeps into sand, add more until wax is $\frac{1}{8}$ inch from rim. Let wax cool 2 hours. Wax will shrink, forming well near center. Poke hole in wax skin using skewer, and fill well with melted wax. Allow wax to cool 1 hour.

7. Push wick through center of well. Use skewer to create hole, if necessary. Tie opposite end of wick to chopstick and lay chopstick across sand.

8. Let candle set 3 to 4 hours or overnight.

9. Untie wick from chopstick and lift candle out of sand, brushing off excess and smoothing outside surface.

10. Trim wick to $\frac{1}{2}$ inch, using scissors. Alternately stand candle on its bottom and top for 2 to 3 seconds at a time in top half of double boiler over boiling water; this process will melt down wax slightly to smooth out any rough surfaces.

Multi-wick with Fragrance

If you have seen the elegant multi-wick candles that decorate the showrooms of today's fashion designers, you have probably wondered how you could ever justify spending the money when these sleek candles appear so simple to make. Wonder no more. The method is a simple one: position the wicks, add fragrance to the wax, and pour into the mold.

YOU WILL NEED:

Empty paper milk container with wax

coating, 1-quart size, cleaned and dried

Scissors

Packing tape with nylon threads,

2 inches wide

Nonstick cooking spray

Awl

3 primed square braid wicks, each 6 inches

long, for candle 2 to 4 inches in diame-

ter (see instructions for priming wicks

on page 61)

3 metal washers

1. Open up pour-spout section of milk container. Cut along folds to create four flaps, using scissors. Cut off one flap and adjacent long panel (see diagram A). Place container, open-side up, on flat surface. Overlap two opposite flaps. Then, fold up remaining flap to seal side of container (see diagram B). Reinforce all exterior sides using bands of tape.

2. Apply light coat of nonstick spray to interior walls and floor of container.

3. Turn mold over and use awl to poke three holes in bottom: one in center position, one $2\frac{1}{4}$ inches to the left of center hole, and one $2\frac{1}{4}$ inches to right of center hole (see diagram C).

4. Tie one end of wick to washer (as in diagram C). Repeat with other wicks and washers.

(continued on page 104)

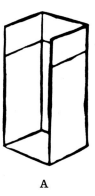

A

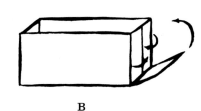

B

(continued from page 102)

Mold sealer

3 chopsticks

4 bricks

Double boiler

$3^3/_4$ teaspoons stearin

1 tablet wax dye (more or less to

acheive desired shade) in pink,

or color as desired

Wooden spoon

$2^1/_2$ pounds paraffin wax,

melting point 140°F

Candy thermometer

Fragrance oil

Ladle with lip

Scissors

5. Thread opposite end of each wick through one hole at underside of mold, securing washer to mold using mold sealer. Position mold right-side up on flat surface. Lay one chopstick on top of mold above one wick. Pull up free end of wick in corresponding position, and tie wick to chopstick. Repeat with remaining wicks (as in diagram D). Lean bricks against outside walls of mold to reinforce.

6. Boil water in bottom half of double boiler.

7. Melt stearin and wax dye together in top half of double boiler. Stir until blended, using wooden spoon. Add paraffin wax and heat until mixture reaches about 155°F on candy thermometer. Do not let wax get hotter than 165°F.

8. When mixture reaches desired temperature, turn off heat. Stir in 10 drops of fragrance oil. Tilt mold and use ladle to pour wax onto the interior wall; then stand mold upright and continue to fill until wax is $^1/_8$ inch from rim. Let wax cool 1 hour. Wax will shrink, forming well near wick. Poke hole in wax skin using skewer, and fill well with melted wax. Allow to cool 1 hour. Repeat process as necessary.

9. Untie wicks from chopsticks and clip off washers from bottom of mold. Unmold candle and let set 3 to 4 hours or overnight.

10. Trim away excess bottom wicks and trim top wicks to $^1/_2$ inch.

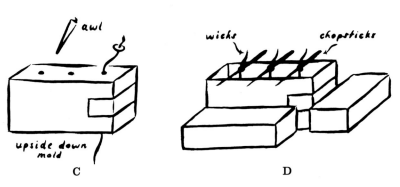

C   D

Technical Glossary | *Glossary of Terms*

The following words and terms are defined according to *Merriam Webster's Collegiate Dictionary, Tenth Edition*, and are interpreted according to the scope of the work. For more information on any of the following, consult larger references dedicated to the subject.

acrylic paint: a water-soluble pigment made from acrylic resin that can be used to decorate wax surfaces. Mixed with dish-washing liquid, acrylic paint adheres well to wax. Can be applied with a brush, sponge, or rag.

beeswax: a natural substance derived from the combs of bees; available in flat sheets with either a smooth or a honeycomb texture; and in natural shades of brown, as well as white, a bleached and filtered variety. When added to paraffin wax, beeswax produces longer-burning candles; when used in molded candles in quantities greater than 10 percent of the wax blend, wax becomes sticky and candle requires a release agent to facilitate removal from mold.

burnish: to smooth a surface and bring up its sheen by rubbing with a polishing tool or material such as a spoon or wad of nylon stocking.

candy thermometer: a heat-sensitive measuring device that indicates the temperature of hot liquids without breaking; can be used to monitor the high melting temperatures of candy and liquid wax.

cavity: the well that forms around the wick of a candle as the melted wax shrinks when it cools and hardens; caused by the contraction of wax as it cools; skin must be punctured and additional melted wax added to eliminate well.

collage: an art form where a collection of seemingly unrelated materials are arranged in an orderly pattern on a background material.

diamond dust: a commercial preparation composed of extra-fine crystal chips that adhere to wax surface and add sparkling patina.

dishwashing liquid: a substance that breaks down the surface tension of water and water-based paints such as acrylic paint used in painting candles. Increases adhesion between paint and wax.

double boiler: a two-part cooking vessel in which one pot nests inside another; the bottom pot is filled with water and placed over a live burner, causing the water to heat up, usually to boiling. When used to melt wax in candle making, the boiling water transfers heat to the wax contents in the top pot so that the wax safely melts without burning.

fragrance: pleasant scent in liquid form added by a dropper to candle wax in its molten state.

glaze: to spray or dip a candle in liquid wax to provide a smooth protective coating for a wax substratum.

gold leaf: thin-gauge metal sheets composed of several elements; also called "composition gold leaf"and "Dutch metal."

grid: a framework organized into parallel lines drawn at even intervals and in perpendicular orientation to one another. Used to map out position of color tiles for mosaic pattern.

heat gun: a hand-held heat dispenser that emanates focused heat; can be used to melt outermost layer of candle for better paper adhesion.

high-tack white glue: a thick, nontoxic white adhesive with a pasty consistency that is used to make wax surface more adherent to gold leaf; also used to join porous materials to wax (i.e., paper mosaic tiles); dries at a faster rate than white glue and usually does not warp paper unless applied in thick coats.

malleable: the property of being capable of molded, bent, or hammered without breaking.

masking tape: an adhesive strip that comes in rolls; available in a variety of adhesive grades from low-tack to high-tack; used to mask designs on candles.

metal stamp: a decorative plate made of metal possessing a raised monogram or line drawing.

metal washer: hardware item used to weight wicks at underside of molds.

mold: a hollow vessel with closed bottom and open top that houses a wick and melted wax that, when hardened and released, becomes a candle of the exact shape, size, and character of the mold; made from cardboard, wood, metal, or acrylic. Common three-dimensional shapes are pyramid, oblique triangle, round, square, scalloped, star, moon, and heart.
 acrylic molds: manufactured in one piece so that there are no seam marks. They are clear so that all stages of the candle-making process are visible.
 metal molds: metal seam on mold creates seam mark on candle; use mineral spirits to smooth wax, and burnish with wad of nylon stocking. Designer tip: molds

should be warmed before melted wax is poured in, to produce candle with smoother finish.

mold sealer: a reusable putty-like substance with elastic properties that acts like a gasket, sealing the areas of the mold where wax can seep (i.e., the wick hole and base seams); also makes molds watertight.

overdipping: a process of submerging a ready-made candle in wax to seal the substrate, and to increase the sheen and smoothness of the candle; also called glazing.

paint marker: a pen that dispenses liquid paint through its felt tip; suited for use directly on wax surfaces. Pumping action starts paint flow.

paraffin wax: a distillate of wood, coal, or petroleum used in candle making; solid at room temperature, paraffin melts to a liquid state when exposed to heat. Available in four grades or melting points: 129°F, which works well with container-type candles and votives; 139°F, which is good for overdipping; 140°F, which works well with rubber, plastic, and metal molds, and also for free-form candles; and 145°F, which works well when dipping tapers since it is characterized by good adhesion between wax layers. Sold in 10- to 11-pound slabs that, when melted, yield about 4 quarts of liquid wax.

primed wick: a length of cotton wick that has been soaked in and coated with melted wax and allowed to harden, making it stiff; facilitates the insertion of the wick into the wick holes in molds.

Pyrex measuring cup: a glass container with spout and handle used for holding and pouring hot liquids; easily conducts heat.

raffia: the fiber from the leaves of a tree growing in Madagascar; used as a decorative tie.

Rub 'n Buff: a commercial paint in cream form that is applied directly to the wax by rubbing; confers a metallic sheen to the wax surface; available in 5-ounce tubes in white, silver, copper, and gold.

rubber stamp: a hand-held printing tool with rubber pad containing the lines of design or motif in relief that, when loaded with ink from an ink pad, can be pressed onto a flat surface, leaving an imprint.

scent: commercially prepared fragrances for use in candle making.

sealing wax: a wax blend that is heated to a liquid state and applied in drops to produce surface decoration; suited to embossing using metal stamps and rubber stamps; available in chunks or sticks with wicks in such colors as burgundy, gold, black, silver, and red.

shapes: the three-dimensional configurations of candles of any description; in molded candle, the container determines the size, shape, and character of the poured wax candle (i.e., cylinders); in free-hand manipulations of wax, candles have a more narrow range of shape (i.e., rolled beeswax candles).

stearin: a wax additive in powder form that, when added to paraffin wax, raises the melting point of the wax so that it produces a harder candle. It increases the shrinkage of wax so that wax candle releases more easily from mold. It produces a candle that is more opaque and less translucent. It also darkens the color of candle wax when dye is used to color the paraffin. Ratio is 10 percent stearin to 90 percent paraffin wax. It is important to always melt and mix stearin with dye before adding wax to mixture.

temperature: the degree of heat contained in a substance measured by a thermometer; energy needed to melt wax into liquid state for pouring; see melting temperatures cited under paraffin.

translucent crystals: wax additive used primarily in overdipping and glazing techniques; maintains clarity and promotes hardness of wax; also referred to by commercial name Clear Sheen.

wax: see *paraffin wax* and *beeswax*.

wax dye: tablets, powders, or liquids used to add color to plain wax. The amount of dye determines the shade of wax, as does the number of layers of colored wax applied to the candle; the color of dyed wax in the molten state is often different from dyed wax in the solid, cold state. To test wax for the shade of color, dip the end of a stick or spoon in dyed wax and allow a drop to fall on white paper. The resulting shade will be slightly lighter than the actual color on candle; multiple coats will darken the shade.

wicks: braided strands of cotton thread that come in small, large, and extra-large diameters; provide the connection between the vapor from the burning wax and the flame. Generally, small wicks are suited to candles that have a diameter of 2 inches or less; large wicks are suited to those candles between 2 inches and 4 inches in diameter; and extra-large wicks are suited to those candles with diameters of 4 inches or more.

wicks, square braid: wicks suited for dipped and molded candles. Flat braid wicks are suited for rolled candles; papercore and wire-core are suited for container-type candles. If the wick is too small, it will go out or cause the candle to drip; if the wick is too thick, it will smoke.

wick end: the section of the wick that is inserted through the wick hole and allowed to extend beyond the barrier formed by the mold; becomes the end that is lighted with a match.

wick hole: an opening through which a wick is inserted; usually positioned at the underside of the candle mold.

wick pin: a metal tool used to create a wick hole in free-form candles, especially votive candles.

wick tab: a metal disk that holds a wick in place; used in short candles, and placed on the base of the candle mold, especially votives. Tab can be square or round with "X"cut into center so that wick can be inserted and held securely; suited for molds with no wick hole or for container-type candles.

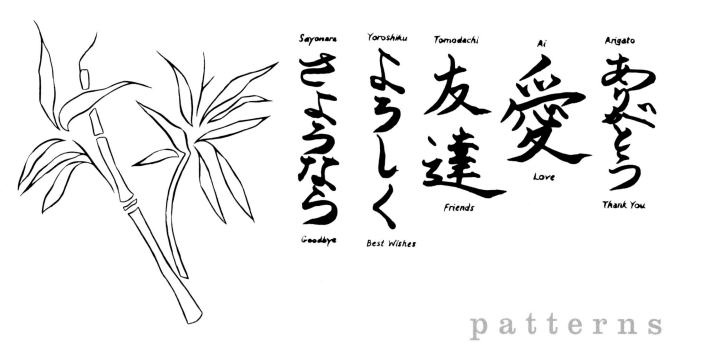

Sayonara

さようなら

Goodbye

Yoroshiku

よろしく

Best Wishes

Tomodachi

友達

Friends

Ai

愛

Love

Arigato

ありがとう

Thank You

patterns

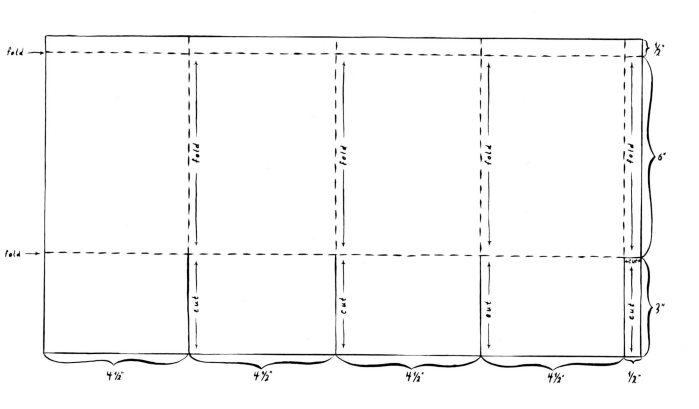

source list

Barker Company
15106 10th Avenue Southwest
Seattle, WA 98166
800.543.0601
www.barkerco.com

Bath and Bodyworks
800.395.1001

Bridge Kitchenware
214 East 52nd Street
New York, NY 10022
212.688.4220

Crate and Barrel
800.323.5461

Flickers
954.525.6687

Glory Bee
120 North Seneca
Eugene, OR 97402
800.456.7923
www.glorybee.com
sales@glorybee.com (e-mail)

Honey Wax
800.880.7694

IKEA
800.434.4532 (catalog)

New York Cake and Baking Supply Company
212.675.2253

Pearl Paint
308 Canal Street
New York, NY 10013
212.431.7932

Pier 1
800.447.4371

Pottery Barn
800.922.5507 (catalog)

Pourette
1418 NW 53rd Street
Seattle, WA 98107
800.888.9425
www.pourette.com

Walnut Hill Company
P.O. Box 599
Green Lane and Wilson Avenue
Bristol, PA 19007
215.785.6511
www.walnuthillco.com

index